This is **Me**

WHAT A WONDERFUL PERSON I AM !

I can look.

I can walk.

I can stand.

I can run.

I can jump.

Sometimes I fall.

Ouch!

Be brave!

And sometimes I cry if I'm hurt.

LOOK WHAT I CAN DO.

I can listen.

I can talk.

I can see.

I can smell.

8

I can touch.

I can eat. Yum!

And when I sleep,
I have nice
dreams.

I can wash myself.

I'M NO LONGER A BABY.

comb

brush

I can comb myself.

soap

I can take a bath by myself.

towel

water

10

I can brush my teeth.

toothpaste

I always put my things away neatly.
Mommy likes that.

Mommy has taught
me to sew on buttons...

... and how to make
my bed all by myself!

I have a head.

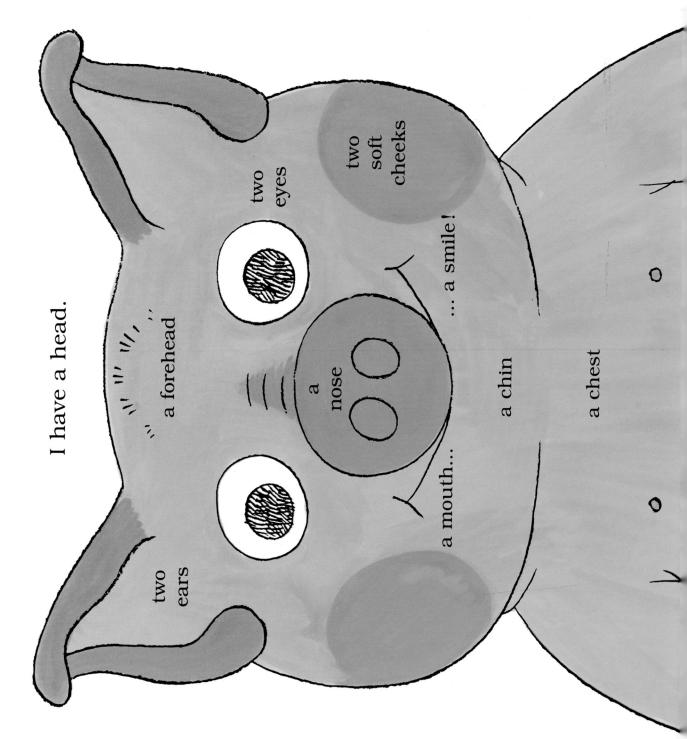

two ears

a forehead

two eyes

two soft cheeks

a nose

... a smile!

a mouth...

a chin

a chest

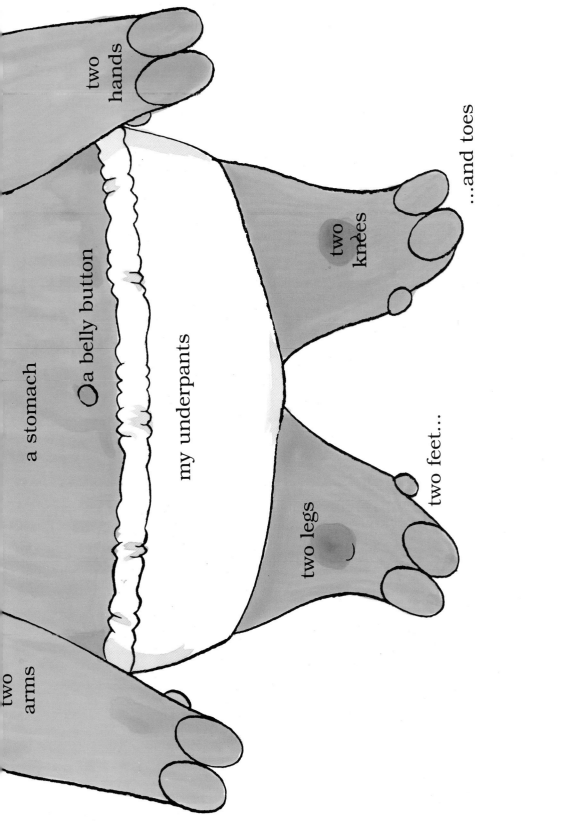

two hands

two arms

a stomach

a belly button

my underpants

two legs

two knees

two feet...

...and toes

THIS IS ME FROM THE FRONT.

13

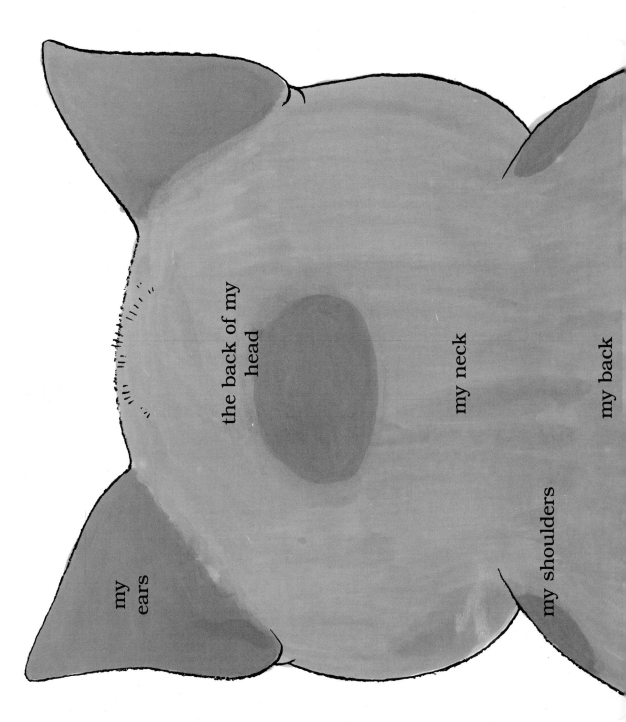

my
ears

the back of my
head

my neck

my shoulders

my back

14

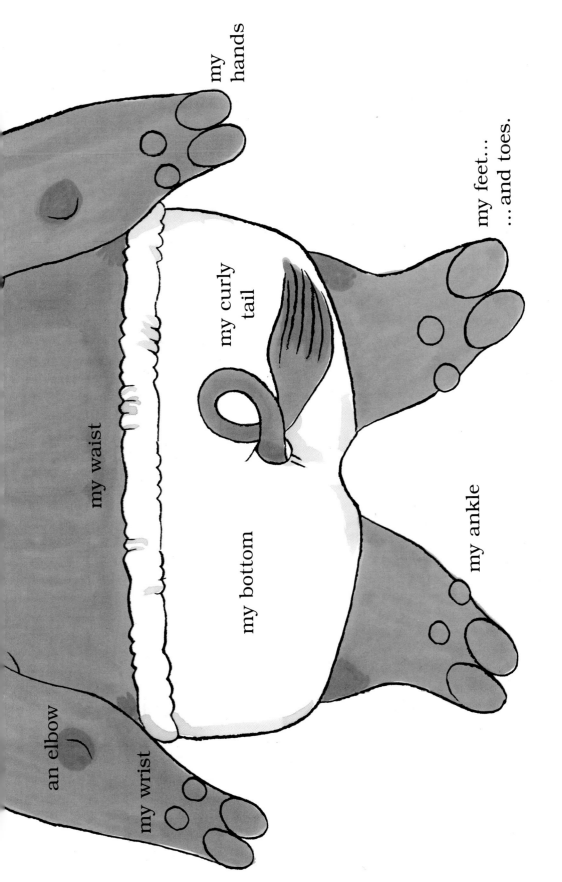

my hands

my feet...
...and toes.

my waist

my curly
tail

my bottom

my ankle

an elbow

my wrist

**THIS IS ME
FROM BEHIND.**

15

LOOK AT ALL MY CLOTHES.

shirt

blazer

overcoat

jacket

overalls

sweater

vest

undershirt

underpants

sneakers

belt

socks

wrist watch

blue jeans

dress

skirt

blouse

bonnet

purse

tights

handbag

hair comb

sunhat

headband

necklace

earrings

ring

I CAN DRESS MYSELF.

closet

Hey! That's no way to put on your shorts!

suspenders

coat hanger

socks

cap

bathrobe

18

When I go to
a party, I get
dressed up.

bow tie

handkerchief

necktie

I bring flowers
as a gift.

slippers

sandals

pajamas

nightie

When I go to bed at night,
this is what I wear.

I DRESS DIFFERENTLY
FOR ALL KINDS OF WEATHER.

In winter, I dress for the cold.

earmuffs

mittens

wool hat

gloves

ski jacket

snowsuit

my sled

scarf

ice skates

When it rains, I dress to keep dry.

rainhat

umbrella

raincoat

boots

puddle

rubbers

In summer, at the beach, this is what I wear :

sunhat

sunglasses

swimsuit